LEAD WITH HONOR

U.S. Army Ranger leadership principales
and how to use them in every day life

John Moore

This book is dedicated to the love of my life, the person that has stuck by me through "Thick & Thin"

I love you,
Sophia Zewdu

CONTENTS

Introduction:

Leadership is a crucial skill that can make or break an individual's success in both personal and professional endeavors. The U.S. Army Rangers are renowned for their effective leadership techniques and tactics, which have been refined through years of rigorous training and experience. In this book, we will explore the key principles that underpin U.S. Army Ranger leadership and demonstrate how they can be applied to everyday life.

Through a series of 15 chapters, we will delve into various aspects of Ranger leadership, including decision-making, communication, adaptability, and resilience. Drawing on examples from both military and civilian contexts, we will examine how these principles can be used to enhance personal and professional effectiveness, build stronger relationships, and achieve greater success.

Whether you are a student, a business professional, or simply seeking to improve your leadership skills, this book will provide you with practical insights and strategies to help you lead with honor, integrity, and purpose.

CHAPTER 1: LEADERSHIP

Leadership is an essential aspect of life, both personal and professional. It is the ability to inspire and guide others towards a common goal, to influence and motivate people towards achieving their full potential. While many individuals possess leadership qualities, only a few have the skills to become great leaders.

One group that embodies the principles of exceptional leadership is the United States Army Rangers. The Rangers are an elite special operations force within the U.S. Army that specializes in direct-action operations, reconnaissance, and counter-terrorism. The Army Rangers undergo rigorous training and are held to the highest standards of leadership and integrity.

The leadership principles of the U.S. Army Rangers are not only relevant to military operations, but they can also be applied in everyday life. These principles can help individuals develop their leadership skills, communicate effectively, build strong teams, make tough decisions, and navigate challenges.

In this book, we will explore the U.S. Army Ranger leadership principles and how to use them in everyday life. We will examine the essential elements of leadership, including self-awareness, goal-setting, effective communication, team building, integrity, decision-making, trust, and credibility, among others.

Throughout each chapter, we will provide practical examples, tools, and strategies for applying these principles to your personal and professional life. By the end of this book, you will have a clear understanding of how to incorporate the U.S. Army Ranger leadership principles into your life and become a more effective leader.

Leadership is not limited to the battlefield or the boardroom; it is a critical component of everyday life. Whether you are a student, an employee, a parent, or a community member, you can benefit from developing your leadership skills. The U.S. Army Ranger leadership principles are an excellent foundation for any individual seeking to enhance their leadership abilities.

In the next chapter, we will explore the importance of self-awareness in leadership and provide practical strategies for developing self-awareness.

CHAPTER 2: SELF-AWARENESS

Self-awareness is the foundation of effective leadership. It involves understanding your strengths and weaknesses, your values and beliefs, and how your behavior and communication impact others. A self-aware leader is better equipped to make sound decisions, manage conflicts, and build strong relationships with their team members.

In this chapter, we will explore the importance of self-awareness in leadership and provide practical strategies for developing self-awareness.

The first step in developing self-awareness is to assess your strengths and weaknesses. It is essential to understand your strengths and leverage them to achieve your goals, while also recognizing your weaknesses and taking steps to improve them. One effective way to assess your strengths and weaknesses is to solicit feedback from others, including colleagues, friends, and family members. Ask them to identify your strengths and areas for improvement, and use this feedback to develop a plan for personal growth.

Another critical aspect of self-awareness is understanding your values and beliefs. Your values and beliefs shape your behavior and influence your decision-making. Take the time to reflect on what is most important to you, and how your values and beliefs impact your leadership style. By aligning your values with your actions, you can inspire trust and build credibility with your team.

Effective communication is another key component of self-awareness. It is essential to understand how your communication style impacts others and adjust your approach accordingly. One effective way to improve communication is to practice active listening. Active listening involves focusing on the speaker, asking clarifying questions, and summarizing the speaker's points to ensure you understand their perspective.

Finally, it is essential to be aware of your emotions and how they impact your behavior. Emotional intelligence is the ability to recognize and manage your emotions, as well as the emotions of others. By developing emotional intelligence, you can build stronger relationships, manage conflicts, and lead with empathy.

In summary, self-awareness is critical to effective leadership. By understanding your strengths and weaknesses, values and beliefs, communication style, and emotional intelligence, you can become a more effective leader. In the next chapter, we will explore the importance of setting goals and provide practical strategies for setting SMART goals.

CHAPTER 3:
SETTING GOALS

Leaders who are successful in achieving their goals are more likely to inspire their team members to do the same. Setting goals provides direction and focus, and helps leaders stay motivated and accountable. In this chapter, we will explore the importance of setting goals and provide practical strategies for setting SMART goals.

SMART is an acronym for Specific, Measurable, Achievable, Relevant, and Time-bound. When setting goals, it is essential to ensure they meet these criteria. Specific goals are clear and concise, and have a defined outcome. Measurable goals are quantifiable, and progress can be tracked over time. Achievable goals are challenging but realistic, and within the realm of possibility. Relevant goals are aligned with your values and priorities, and relevant to your role as a leader. Time-bound goals have a set deadline or timeframe for completion.

When setting goals, it is essential to involve your team members in the process. By involving them, you can ensure that the goals are aligned with the team's objectives and priorities. You can also create buy-in and increase motivation by involving your team in the goal-setting process.

Another important aspect of goal setting is to break down larger goals into smaller, more manageable milestones. By breaking down goals into smaller chunks, you can track progress and stay motivated as you achieve each milestone. This approach can also make larger goals feel less overwhelming and more achievable.

It is also important to ensure that your goals are aligned with your organization's vision and mission. By aligning your goals with the larger organizational objectives, you can ensure that you are contributing to the overall success of the organization. This approach can also create a sense of purpose and meaning for you and your team members.

Finally, it is important to regularly review and adjust your goals. Goals should be reviewed on a regular basis, and adjusted as necessary to reflect changes in priorities, resources, or circumstances. By regularly reviewing your goals, you can ensure that they remain relevant and aligned with the larger organizational objectives.

In summary, setting SMART goals is an essential aspect of effective leadership. By involving your team members in the process, breaking down larger goals into smaller milestones, aligning goals with organizational objectives, and regularly reviewing and adjusting goals, you can become a more effective leader. In the next chapter, we will explore the importance of effective communication and provide practical strategies for improving communication skills.

CHAPTER 4: EFFECTIVE COMMUNICATION

Effective communication is a critical component of successful leadership. Leaders who can communicate effectively can build trust, inspire action, and achieve their goals. In this chapter, we will explore the importance of effective communication and provide practical strategies for improving your communication skills.

Communication can take many forms, including verbal, nonverbal, and written. Verbal communication includes speaking and listening, while nonverbal communication includes body language and facial expressions. Written communication includes emails, memos, and reports. Effective communication involves all of these forms of communication, and requires that you understand and use each form effectively.

One important aspect of effective communication is active listening. Active listening involves fully focusing on the speaker, taking time to understand their perspective, and responding in a thoughtful and respectful manner. Active listening can help build trust, improve relationships, and prevent misunderstandings.

Another important aspect of effective communication is clarity. Clear communication involves using language that is easy to understand, avoiding jargon and technical terms, and using examples and analogies to illustrate your point. Clarity can help ensure that your message is received and understood by your audience.

Nonverbal communication is also an essential aspect of effective communication. Nonverbal communication includes body language, facial expressions, and tone of voice. It can convey a wide range of emotions, and can either reinforce or contradict verbal communication. By being aware of your nonverbal communication, you can ensure that your message is consistent with your intended meaning.

Written communication is another important aspect of effective communication. When writing, it is essential to be clear and concise, and to use language that is appropriate for your audience. Emails and memos should be structured in a way that is easy to read and understand, and should include a clear call to action.

Finally, it is essential to tailor your communication style to your audience. Different audiences may have different communication preferences and styles, and it is important to be aware of these differences and adapt your communication style accordingly.

In summary, effective communication is an essential aspect of successful leadership. By actively listening, being clear and concise, being aware of your nonverbal communication, and tailoring your communication style to your audience, you can become a more effective communicator. In the next chapter, we will explore the importance of teamwork and provide practical strategies for building effective teams.

CHAPTER 5: BUILDING EFFECTIVE TEAMS

As an Army Ranger, you are trained to operate as part of a team. Building and leading effective teams is a critical skill for success in the military, and in many other fields as well. In this chapter, we will explore the importance of teamwork and provide practical strategies for building and leading effective teams.

Teamwork is essential in any organization that involves multiple individuals working towards a common goal. Effective teams are able to work together seamlessly, leveraging each team member's strengths and compensating for weaknesses. They are able to communicate effectively, resolve conflicts, and adapt to changing circumstances.

One key to building effective teams is to ensure that team members share a common understanding of the team's goals and objectives. This can be achieved through clear communication, setting goals that are specific, measurable, achievable, relevant, and time-bound (SMART), and ensuring that each team member understands their role and responsibilities.

Another important aspect of building effective teams is to establish a culture of trust and mutual respect. This can be achieved by promoting open and honest communication, recognizing and valuing each team member's contributions, and addressing conflicts in a respectful and constructive manner.

Effective teams also require strong leadership. Leaders of effective teams must be able to inspire and motivate their team members, set a positive example, and make difficult decisions when necessary. They must also be able to delegate tasks and responsibilities, and trust their team members to execute them effectively.

Finally, it is important to continuously assess and adapt the team's strategies and processes to ensure that they are effective. This may involve soliciting feedback from team members, measuring and evaluating team performance, and making adjustments as necessary.

In summary, building and leading effective teams is a critical skill for success in any field. By establishing clear goals and objectives, promoting a culture of trust and respect, providing strong leadership, and continuously assessing and adapting strategies and processes, you can build and lead effective teams that are able to achieve their goals and objectives. In the next chapter, we will explore the importance of adaptability and provide practical strategies for developing this critical skill.

CHAPTER 6: DEVELOPING ADAPTABILITY

Adaptability is a critical skill in the U.S. Army Ranger training and in life. Adaptability is the ability to adjust to new situations, learn new skills, and overcome challenges. In this chapter, we will explore the importance of adaptability and provide practical strategies for developing this critical skill.

In the Army Ranger training, soldiers are trained to operate in a variety of environments, from the dense jungles to the arid deserts. This requires soldiers to be able to adapt quickly to new situations and environments. Similarly, in life, we are often faced with unexpected challenges and changes that require us to adapt quickly.

One key to developing adaptability is to be open to new experiences and perspectives. This means being willing to try new things, learn new skills, and approach problems from different angles. It also means being willing to listen to others and consider their perspectives, even if they differ from your own.

Another important aspect of developing adaptability is to maintain a positive attitude and mindset. This means being resilient in the face of setbacks and failures, and viewing challenges as opportunities for growth and learning. It also means being able to stay focused and productive in uncertain or changing circumstances.

Effective problem-solving skills are also important for developing adaptability. This involves breaking down complex problems into smaller, more manageable components, identifying potential solutions, and evaluating the strengths and weaknesses of each option. It also involves being willing to pivot and adjust your approach as needed, based on new information or changing circumstances.

Finally, building a strong support network can also help to develop adaptability. This includes surrounding yourself with positive and supportive people, seeking out mentors and role models, and cultivating relationships that are based on trust and mutual respect.

In summary, adaptability is a critical skill for success in the Army Ranger training and in life. By being open to new experiences and perspectives, maintaining a positive attitude and mindset, developing effective problem-solving skills, and building a strong support network, you can develop the adaptability you need to thrive in any situation. In the next chapter, we will explore the importance of resilience and provide practical strategies for developing this critical skill.

CHAPTER 7: BUILDING RESILIENCE

Resilience is the ability to recover quickly from setbacks, adapt to change, and cope with stress and adversity. In the U.S. Army Ranger training, resilience is essential for success in the face of challenging physical and mental demands. In this chapter, we will explore the importance of resilience and provide practical strategies for building this critical skill.

Resilience involves a combination of mental, emotional, and physical toughness. This means being able to stay focused and motivated in the face of adversity, maintain a positive attitude and mindset, and take care of your physical health and well-being.

One key to building resilience is to cultivate a growth mindset. This means viewing challenges and setbacks as opportunities for growth and learning, rather than as failures. It also means embracing a lifelong learning mindset and seeking out opportunities to develop new skills and knowledge.

Another important aspect of building resilience is to maintain a strong support network. This includes surrounding yourself with positive and supportive people who can offer encouragement, guidance, and advice. It also means being willing to ask for help when you need it and offering support to others in return.

Effective stress-management strategies are also important for building resilience. This involves developing healthy coping mechanisms for managing stress, such as exercise, meditation, or talking to a trusted friend or counselor. It also involves maintaining a healthy work-life balance, prioritizing self-care, and setting realistic goals and expectations for yourself.

Finally, it is important to maintain a strong sense of purpose and meaning in your life. This involves identifying your values, passions, and goals, and working towards them with dedication and perseverance. It also means finding ways to give back to your community and make a positive impact on the world around you.

In summary, building resilience is essential for success in the U.S. Army Ranger training and in life. By cultivating a growth mindset, maintaining a strong support network, developing effective stress-management strategies, and maintaining a strong sense of purpose and meaning, you can build the resilience you need to overcome challenges and thrive in any situation. In the next chapter, we will explore the importance of effective communication and provide practical strategies for improving your communication skills.

CHAPTER 8: EFFECTIVE COMMUNICATION

Effective communication is critical for success in the U.S. Army Ranger training and in life. Communication skills enable you to convey your thoughts, ideas, and needs clearly and effectively, as well as to listen and understand others. In this chapter, we will explore the importance of effective communication and provide practical strategies for improving your communication skills.

One key to effective communication is active listening. This involves paying close attention to what the other person is saying, both verbally and nonverbally, and demonstrating that you understand their perspective. This can involve asking clarifying questions, summarizing their points, and providing feedback.

Another important aspect of effective communication is clear and concise messaging. This involves conveying your thoughts and ideas in a way that is easy to understand and free from ambiguity or confusion. It can involve organizing your thoughts before speaking, using clear and simple language, and avoiding jargon or technical terms that may not be familiar to the listener.

Nonverbal communication is also critical to effective communication. This includes body language, facial expressions, and tone of voice. By being aware of your nonverbal cues and actively managing them, you can convey confidence, assertiveness, and professionalism.

Effective communication also involves adapting your communication style to the needs of the situation and the audience. This can involve adjusting your language, tone, and style to match the communication preferences of the listener, as well as to the context of the communication.

Finally, it is important to practice effective communication skills regularly. This can involve seeking out opportunities for public speaking, engaging in difficult conversations, and soliciting feedback from others to identify areas for improvement.

In summary, effective communication is a critical skill for success in the U.S. Army Ranger training and in life. By practicing active listening, clear and concise messaging, effective nonverbal communication, and adapting to the needs of the situation and audience, you can become a more effective communicator and achieve your goals. In the next chapter, we will explore the importance of goal-setting and provide practical strategies for setting and achieving your goals.

CHAPTER 9: GOAL-SETTING

Goal-setting is a critical component of success in the U.S. Army Ranger training and in life. Goals provide direction, motivation, and a sense of purpose, helping you to stay focused and on track. In this chapter, we will explore the importance of goal-setting and provide practical strategies for setting and achieving your goals.

One key to effective goal-setting is setting SMART goals. SMART goals are Specific, Measurable, Achievable, Relevant, and Time-bound. This involves setting goals that are clear and specific, measurable and quantifiable, achievable and realistic, relevant to your overall objectives, and time-bound with a specific deadline.

Another important aspect of goal-setting is identifying and prioritizing your goals. This can involve making a list of your goals, categorizing them by priority, and identifying the specific steps you need to take to achieve each goal.

It is also important to create a plan of action for achieving your goals. This involves breaking down your goals into smaller, manageable tasks, identifying any obstacles or challenges you may face, and creating a timeline for completing each task.

Accountability is another key component of goal-setting. This can involve sharing your goals with others, finding an accountability partner, or regularly tracking and reviewing your progress towards your goals.

Finally, it is important to celebrate your successes and learn from your failures. Celebrating your successes can help to reinforce positive behaviors and motivate you to continue striving towards your goals. Learning from your failures can help you to identify areas for improvement and adjust your approach for future success.

In summary, goal-setting is a critical skill for success in the U.S. Army Ranger training and in life. By setting SMART goals, identifying and prioritizing your goals, creating a plan of action, being accountable, and celebrating successes and learning from failures, you can achieve your goals and reach your full potential. In the next chapter, we will explore the importance of resilience and provide practical strategies for building resilience.

CHAPTER 10: RESILIENCE

Resilience is the ability to bounce back from adversity and to adapt to changing circumstances. In the U.S. Army Ranger training, resilience is a critical skill for survival and success in the face of challenges and obstacles. In this chapter, we will explore the importance of resilience and provide practical strategies for building resilience.

One key to building resilience is maintaining a positive attitude. This involves focusing on the positive aspects of a situation, reframing negative thoughts into positive ones, and developing a sense of optimism and hopefulness. By maintaining a positive attitude, you can increase your ability to cope with stress and adversity.

Another important aspect of resilience is developing a strong support network. This can involve seeking support from family, friends, colleagues, or mental health professionals. By building a strong support network, you can increase your ability to cope with stress and adversity and develop a sense of connectedness and belonging.

It is also important to engage in self-care practices to build resilience. This can involve engaging in regular exercise, getting enough sleep, practicing mindfulness or meditation, and engaging in hobbies or activities that bring you joy and fulfillment. By engaging in self-care practices, you can increase your overall well-being and build your capacity for resilience.

Another important aspect of building resilience is developing problem-solving skills. This involves identifying problems or challenges, breaking them down into smaller, manageable tasks, and developing a plan of action for solving the problem. By developing problem-solving skills, you can increase your ability to cope with stress and adversity and develop a sense of self-efficacy and confidence.

Finally, it is important to learn from past experiences to build resilience. This involves reflecting on past experiences, identifying what worked well and what didn't, and developing a plan for how to approach similar situations in the future. By learning from past experiences, you can increase your ability to cope with stress and adversity and develop a sense of resilience and adaptability.

In summary, resilience is a critical skill for survival and success in the U.S. Army Ranger training and in life. By maintaining a positive attitude, building a strong support network, engaging in self-care practices, developing problem-solving skills, and learning from past experiences, you can build your capacity for resilience and adaptability. In the next chapter, we will explore the importance of teamwork and provide practical strategies for building effective teams.

CHAPTER 11: BUILDING TEAMWORK

In the U.S. Army Ranger training, teamwork is essential for mission success. Effective teams work together to accomplish goals, solve problems, and support each other in the face of challenges and obstacles. In this chapter, we will explore the importance of teamwork and provide practical strategies for building effective teams.

One key to building effective teams is establishing clear goals and objectives. This involves setting specific, measurable, attainable, relevant, and time-bound (SMART) goals and communicating them clearly to all team members. By establishing clear goals and objectives, team members can work together toward a common purpose and stay focused on what is important.

Another important aspect of effective teamwork is establishing clear roles and responsibilities. This involves assigning tasks and responsibilities based on individual strengths and expertise, and communicating them clearly to all team members. By establishing clear roles and responsibilities, team members can work together more efficiently and effectively, and avoid confusion or overlap.

Effective communication is also critical for effective teamwork. This involves listening actively, speaking clearly and concisely, and using feedback to improve communication over time. By practicing effective communication, team members can avoid misunderstandings, build trust and respect, and work together more collaboratively.

Collaboration and cooperation are also important aspects of effective teamwork. This involves working together to solve problems, share information, and support each other in the face of challenges and obstacles. By fostering collaboration and cooperation, team members can leverage each other's strengths and expertise, and accomplish more together than they could alone.

Finally, it is important to celebrate successes and learn from failures as a team. This involves recognizing and celebrating individual and team accomplishments, and reflecting on what worked well and what didn't in order to improve performance in the future. By celebrating successes and learning from failures together, team members can build morale and cohesion, and develop a shared sense of purpose and commitment.

In summary, effective teamwork is essential for mission success in the U.S. Army Ranger training and in life. By establishing clear goals and objectives, establishing clear roles and responsibilities, practicing effective communication, fostering collaboration and cooperation, and celebrating successes and learning from failures together, teams can work together more efficiently and effectively, and achieve their goals with greater ease. In the next chapter, we will explore the importance of adaptability and provide practical strategies for building adaptability skills.

CHAPTER 12: ADAPTABILITY

In the U.S. Army Ranger training, adaptability is critical for success. Rangers must be able to adapt to changing circumstances and operate effectively in a wide range of environments and conditions. In this chapter, we will explore the importance of adaptability and provide practical strategies for building adaptability skills.

Adaptability involves being able to adjust to changing circumstances and remain effective in the face of uncertainty and ambiguity. This involves being flexible and open-minded, and being able to think creatively and solve problems in new and innovative ways.

One key to building adaptability skills is developing a growth mindset. This involves believing that abilities and intelligence can be developed through dedication and hard work, and that challenges and failures are opportunities to learn and grow. By developing a growth mindset, Rangers can approach new situations with a sense of curiosity and enthusiasm, and view setbacks as opportunities for growth and improvement.

Another important aspect of adaptability is developing a range of skills and competencies. This involves learning new skills and techniques, and broadening one's knowledge and experience in a variety of areas. By developing a range of skills and competencies, Rangers can be better equipped to adapt to new situations and environments, and can approach challenges with confidence and resilience.

Effective communication is also critical for adaptability. This involves being able to communicate effectively with people from different backgrounds and cultures, and being able to adapt one's communication style to different contexts and situations. By practicing effective communication, Rangers can build rapport and trust with others, and can work more effectively in diverse and changing environments.

Another important aspect of adaptability is being able to manage stress and maintain mental and emotional resilience. This involves developing strategies for coping with stress and uncertainty, and being able to stay calm and focused under pressure. By developing mental and emotional resilience, Rangers can remain effective and focused even in the most challenging and stressful situations.

In summary, adaptability is a critical skill for success in the U.S. Army Ranger training and in life. By developing a growth mindset, broadening one's skills and competencies, practicing effective communication, and developing mental and emotional resilience, Rangers can be better equipped to adapt to changing circumstances and remain effective in a wide range of environments and conditions. In the next chapter, we will explore the importance of self-discipline and provide practical strategies for building self-discipline skills.

CHAPTER 13: SELF-DISCIPLINE

Self-discipline is a key principle of U.S. Army Ranger leadership and is essential for success in the Ranger training and in life. In this chapter, we will explore the importance of self-discipline and provide practical strategies for building self-discipline skills.

Self-discipline involves the ability to control one's impulses, emotions, and actions, and to stay focused on long-term goals and objectives. It requires self-awareness, self-control, and the ability to delay gratification in pursuit of a higher purpose.

One key to building self-discipline skills is setting clear goals and objectives. This involves defining what you want to achieve and creating a plan for how to get there. By setting clear goals and objectives, you can stay focused on what is most important and avoid distractions and temptations that might lead you off course.

Another important aspect of self-discipline is developing healthy habits and routines. This involves creating a structured and disciplined approach to your daily routine, including regular exercise, healthy eating habits, and consistent sleep patterns. By developing healthy habits and routines, you can strengthen your self-discipline muscles and make it easier to stay on track and avoid distractions and temptations.

Effective time management is also critical for self-discipline. This involves setting priorities and managing your time effectively to ensure that you are making progress towards your goals and objectives. By managing your time effectively, you can avoid procrastination and stay focused on what is most important.

Another key to building self-discipline skills is practicing mental and emotional resilience. This involves developing strategies for coping with stress and adversity, and being able to stay calm and focused under pressure. By practicing mental and emotional resilience, you can strengthen your self-discipline muscles and stay on track even in the face of challenges and setbacks.

In summary, self-discipline is a critical skill for success in the U.S. Army Ranger training and in life. By setting clear goals and objectives, developing healthy habits and routines, practicing effective time management, and building mental and emotional resilience, Rangers can strengthen their self-discipline muscles and stay focused on what is most important. In the next chapter, we will explore the importance of teamwork and provide practical strategies for building effective teamwork skills.

CHAPTER 14: TEAMWORK

Teamwork is an essential principle of U.S. Army Ranger leadership and is critical for success in the Ranger training and in military operations. In this chapter, we will explore the importance of teamwork and provide practical strategies for building effective teamwork skills.

Teamwork involves the ability to work collaboratively with others towards a common goal or objective. It requires effective communication, trust, and mutual respect, and involves a willingness to put the needs of the team above individual interests.

One key to building effective teamwork skills is developing strong communication skills. This involves the ability to express ideas clearly and listen actively to others, and to provide constructive feedback and support to team members. By developing strong communication skills, Rangers can build trust and mutual respect among team members, and ensure that everyone is working towards the same goals and objectives.

Another important aspect of effective teamwork is building trust and mutual respect among team members. This involves being reliable and dependable, and following through on commitments and responsibilities. It also involves treating others with respect and dignity, and recognizing the unique strengths and contributions that each team member brings to the table.

Effective teamwork also requires a willingness to put the needs of the team above individual interests. This involves being flexible and adaptable, and being willing to make sacrifices for the good of the team. It also involves being open to feedback and constructive criticism, and being willing to learn and grow from the experiences of others.

Finally, effective teamwork requires a commitment to continuous improvement. This involves setting high standards for performance and holding oneself and others accountable for meeting those standards. It also involves a willingness to learn from mistakes and failures, and to continually seek out new ways to improve individual and team performance.

In summary, effective teamwork is critical for success in the U.S. Army Ranger training and in military operations. By developing strong communication skills, building trust and mutual respect among team members, putting the needs of the team above individual interests, and committing to continuous improvement, Rangers can build effective teamwork skills that will serve them well in any situation.

CHAPTER 15: APPLYING U.S. ARMY RANGER LEADERSHIP PRINCIPLES IN EVERYDAY LIFE

Throughout this book, we have explored the U.S. Army Ranger leadership principles and their application in military operations and Ranger training. However, the principles of Ranger leadership are not just relevant to military settings. In fact, they can be applied in everyday life to help individuals become more effective leaders and achieve their personal and professional goals.

In this chapter, we will explore how the principles of Ranger leadership can be applied in everyday life, and provide practical strategies for putting them into practice.

The first principle of Ranger leadership is to lead by example. In everyday life, this means setting a positive example for others by living with integrity and demonstrating a strong work ethic. It involves taking responsibility for one's actions and decisions, and being willing to make sacrifices to achieve one's goals.

The second principle of Ranger leadership is to prioritize the mission. In everyday life, this means setting clear goals and objectives, and prioritizing them above distractions and competing priorities. It involves developing a clear sense of purpose and direction, and staying focused on what is most important.

The third principle of Ranger leadership is to make sound and timely decisions. In everyday life, this means being able to assess situations quickly and make decisions based on the best available information. It involves being willing to take calculated risks, and being able to adjust one's course when necessary.

The fourth principle of Ranger leadership is to seek and take responsibility for one's actions. In everyday life, this means taking ownership of one's successes and failures, and being accountable for one's actions and decisions. It involves being willing to learn from mistakes and failures, and taking steps to improve one's performance.

The fifth and final principle of Ranger leadership is to maintain physical and mental toughness. In everyday life, this means taking care of oneself physically and mentally, and developing the resilience to overcome challenges and adversity. It involves developing a strong sense of self-discipline and self-control, and being able to persevere through difficult times.

By applying the principles of Ranger leadership in everyday life, individuals can become more effective leaders and achieve their personal and professional goals. Whether one is pursuing a career, building a business, or seeking personal fulfillment, the principles of Ranger leadership can provide a roadmap for success and a framework for personal growth and development.

In conclusion, the principles of U.S. Army Ranger leadership are not just relevant to military settings, but can be applied in everyday life to help individuals become more effective leaders and achieve their goals. By leading by example, prioritizing the mission, making sound and timely decisions, taking responsibility for one's actions, and maintaining physical and mental toughness, individuals can develop the skills and qualities necessary to succeed in any endeavor.

Epilogue:

In conclusion, the U.S. Army Ranger leadership principles are not only applicable to military operations, but also to everyday life. The Ranger Creed, which embodies these principles, serves as a guide for individuals to strive towards excellence, self-discipline, and selfless service.

By incorporating these principles into one's personal and professional life, individuals can develop effective leadership skills, build stronger relationships, and achieve their goals. The Ranger motto, "Rangers lead the way," reminds us to take initiative, be adaptable, and never give up.

Whether you are a civilian, a student, or a member of the military, the Ranger leadership principles can help you become a better leader and make a positive impact in your community. By following the principles of "follow me," "lead by example," and "never quit," you can inspire others to achieve their full potential and create a culture of excellence.

As we look towards the future, let us remember the legacy of the U.S. Army Rangers and their commitment to upholding the values of honor, courage, and commitment. Whether we are facing challenges in our personal or professional lives, we can draw strength from the Ranger Creed and the principles it embodies.

In the words of the Ranger Creed, "I will never leave a fallen comrade to fall into the hands of the enemy, and under no circumstances will I ever embarrass my country." Let us strive to live up to these words and make a positive impact in our world.

The Ranger Creed:

Recognizing that I volunteered as a Ranger, fully knowing the hazards of my chosen profession, I will always endeavor to uphold the prestige, honor, and high esprit de corps of the Rangers.

Acknowledging the fact that a Ranger is a more elite Soldier who arrives at the cutting edge of battle by land, sea, or air, I accept the fact that as a Ranger my country expects me to move further, faster, and fight harder than any other Soldier.

Never shall I fail my comrades. I will always keep myself mentally alert, physically strong, and morally straight, and I will shoulder more than my share of the task, whatever it may be, one hundred percent and then some.

Gallantly will I show the world that I am a specially selected and well-trained Soldier. My courtesy to superior officers, neatness of dress, and care of equipment shall set the example for others to follow.

Energetically will I meet the enemies of my country. I shall defeat them on the field of battle, for I am better trained and will fight with all my might. Surrender is not a Ranger word. I will never leave a fallen comrade to fall into the hands of the enemy and under no circumstances will I ever embarrass my country.

Readily will I display the intestinal fortitude required to fight on to the Ranger objective and complete the mission, though I be the lone survivor.

Rangers lead the way!

Rogers rules for Rangers

The Rogers Rules for Rangers are a set of principles and tactics developed by Major Robert Rogers, the founder of the Rogers'

Rangers, a special unit of colonial troops that operated during the French and Indian War. These rules were later adopted by the U.S. Army Rangers and are still used today. Here are the Rogers Rules for Rangers:

1. Don't forget nothing: This means that Rangers must always be prepared and never forget any aspect of their mission, equipment, or surroundings.

2. Have your musket clean as a whistle, hatchet scoured, sixty rounds powder and ball, and be ready to march at a minute's warning: This rule emphasizes the importance of being well-equipped and ready to move quickly and decisively.

3. When you're on the march, act the way you would if you were sneaking up on a deer: This rule emphasizes the need for stealth and the ability to move silently and unnoticed.

4. See the enemy first: This rule stresses the importance of reconnaissance and the need to gather intelligence before engaging the enemy.

5. Tell the truth about what you see and what you do. There is an army depending on us for correct information. You can lie all you please when you tell other folks about the Rangers, but don't never lie to a Ranger or officer: This rule emphasizes the importance of honesty, especially in reporting intelligence and providing accurate information to superiors.

6. Don't never take a chance you don't have to: This rule emphasizes the need for caution and the importance of minimizing risks.

7. When we're on the march we march single file, far enough apart so one shot can't go through two men: This rule emphasizes the importance of spacing and minimizing the risk of casualties.

8. If we strike swamps, or soft ground, we spread out abreast, so it's hard to track us: This rule emphasizes the need to adapt to the terrain and use it to their advantage.

9. When we march, we keep moving till dark, so as to give the enemy the least possible chance at us: This rule emphasizes the importance of speed and the need to minimize the enemy's opportunity to engage.

10. When we camp, half the party stays awake while the other half sleeps: This rule emphasizes the importance of security and the need to be constantly vigilant.

These rules reflect the principles of the Rangers, including flexibility, adaptability, and initiative, as well as the importance of discipline, preparation, and vigilance.

ABOUT THE AUTHOR

John Moore

 John Moore is a distinguished former U.S. Army Ranger who proudly served our nation for over 20 years. In 2014, he was elected to the Nevada Assembly and served as the vice-chairman of the government affairs committee. He served on the health and human services as well as the elections and legislative operations committees.

John is a multi-talented individual who not only writes books and provides political commentary, but is also in high demand as a public speaker.

A FEW PICTURES OF ME FROM MY DAYS AS A U.S. ARMY RANGER

My Ranger school class picture Class 10-84

White Sands New Mexico 1984

Iraq 2005

Iraq 2005